# COACHING THE
# LITTLE BOYS OF SUMMER

## Fathers, Sons, and the Experience of Youth Baseball

### by Jeff VanHuis

**BASEBALL CONCEPTS**

www.baseball-concepts.com

Black Lake Press

TELL YOUR STORY

BLACKLAKEPRESS.COM

Published by Black Lake Press of Holland, Michigan.
Black Lake Press is a division of Black Lake Studio, LLC.
Direct inquiries to Black Lake Press at www.blacklakepress.com.

ISBN 978-0-9824446-3-4

# Training Package

## Table of Contents

### The Goal

Making youth baseball the best it can be for kids and their parents is what we strive to do. The drills and techniques that we teach are proven to aid in player development and are used by thousands of coaches at every level. This coaches guide contains criteria for what makes a "quality" baseball coach, parent, and player. By learning our roles, together we can all help create a great atmosphere for our Youth Leaguers and the communities they represent. We want to encourage parents to use this baseball product to implement fundamental baseball teachings, as well as an avenue to teach healthy and positive life lessons through the game of baseball. Use the positive quotes section to build a positive practice environment that will make every kid in the league wish they were on your team. All the parents will love you for this. You'll be on your way to being a great coach who makes a wonderful impact in the lives of your players!

Baseball is more than just the great American pastime; it is also a perfect opportunity for dads to be involved in their kids' lives. Parents can bond with their kids while teaching them the game. No matter the age, from the T-ball player to the high school level, baseball can shape character and make life-long memories.

That's the way it was for my dad and I. More than anyone else, he developed my love of the game when I was a little boy. By the time I reached high school, my dad had spent so much time playing baseball with my brother and me, hitting ground balls and catching for us, that the wedding ring he wore on his glove hand developed a flat spot from hours of catching baseballs we threw him over the years.

There are so many wonderful, teachable moments and great stories parents can share with their kids as they spend time playing catch in the back yard after work or on Sunday afternoons. However, it seems that the two things preventing dads and moms from participating in their child's interest in baseball is simply their lack of knowledge of how to practice the game of baseball, and limited confidence in their ability to make it a fun time with their kids. I have provided valuable information on simple and effective ways to become engaged in a game that your child is interested in. My role as a coach and as a father has been to find creative ways to connect with my kids and players on the baseball field while helping them develop as people.

I wrote this book to enhance the quality time that dads spend with their kids working on baseball skills. It seems that almost every boy at one time in his life participates in youth baseball. It might be T-ball, Youth League baseball, or more competitive school leagues, but it seems that the great American pastime is a game that most everyone experiences at one time in their life. My hope is that baseball parents would learn enough about the game that they could help positively coach and mentor their young player. And so, I've shared what I learned over sixteen years as a player and coach into this interactive book. In it, you will find ways for the parent, child, and family bond to be connected while improving the player's baseball skills.

This book is also for parents who become coaches of their child's Youth League team. Whether you have played upper-level baseball in college or are new to the coaching realm, there is something for you in this book. Youth coaches need to start by putting their own ego and selfish ambition aside and focus on learning new tools and ideas that will display that they have a grasp on being the best Youth League dad or coach possible. I want kids to have a positive, constructive experience in Youth League, and at the same time to feel good about their accomplishments. Parents and coaches have an opportunity to help kids grow in their character when by experiencing tough failures as well as exciting successes. This book will show both parents and coaches how to help kids develop these skills in all the areas of youth baseball.

# BASEBALL CONCEPTS' INTRODUCTION

Do not expect that after using this book your team will have an undefeated season or that your child will be in line for a college baseball scholarship. There are no guarantees here. I will teach the ways to instill hard work in your players and motivate you to be a championship dad first, and a coach who cares for kids and makes them the best they can be. It is all about a process of reaching potential. I have learned ways to communicate this to kids, parents, and coaches that can be used in building a team or a child at home. The process of working hard and being focused on the correct way to play the game is what you will get from this book. All of the skills taught in this book are also taught to kids through our quality youth camps. To learn more about our group camps and specific individual position camps, please visit www.baseball-concepts.com.

# Why Baseball?

BASEBALL CONCEPTS

"Things turn out best for people who make the best of the way things turn out."

Many young kids across America and the world become involved with youth baseball. Parents enjoy watching their kids playing Youth League the way they once did, and are happy to have their kids participating in healthy events that will allow them to meet other kids and families. Youth League is a summer legacy that passes from generation to generation, connecting grandpas, dads, and young boys. Whether in the sandlots of the Midwest America or in a revamped, modern East Coast complex, you are sure to find "the little boys of summer" in every community and from every walk of life playing the game of baseball.

Every spring you can find fathers browsing the bat section at local sporting goods stores in search of the latest bat that that will help their future MVP perform. By the large smiles on the faces of the dads, it is clear that they get just as much out of Youth League as the kids do. Warm summer evenings bring carloads of families to Youth League ballparks. It is the most popular youth sport, which generations of families have played and enjoyed together—a great, historic, American tradition.

Why baseball? Baseball seems to teach so many life lessons. As parents, we try hard to teach our kids right from wrong and we preach until we are blue in the face. We have them join play groups in their toddler years to learn how to play and get along with other children. In their adolescent years, parents fret about teaching responsibility and the importance of a good attitude. All of these lessons can be taught in the nine innings of a baseball game. It is a team sport where everyone needs to be dependent on one another and have a positive attitude to make the cohesiveness of the group function—much like those toddler play groups or in ways that a successful corporation would need to in order to function.

Baseball is a game of failure, and far too often kids (and even adults) develop poor attitudes and give up when they encounter tough times in life. If you can handle failing 70% of the time in this game, you will be successful. After all, a .300 hitter is an all-star, a Hall of Fame player. I like this part of baseball, because life isn't about what happens to us, it is all about how we respond to these situations that make us who we are. I love the way baseball teaches this. Baseball is a tricky game of inches, with many random variables, and often times there are situations that we just cannot practice, defend, scout, or avoid. We call these situations "The things that we cannot control." So teaching players to, "Focus on the things that you can control" is the most important mindset. Just like in life, in family re-lationships, we have to focus and practice what we can control and place our time and efforts into this focus. Not worrying about what we have no control over.

It is also important to note that less than one percent of high school seniors will graduate with a full athletic scholarship—and of this less than one percent, only 0.2 percent, will become professional athletes. This statistic is very eye opening. Many parents have a genuine thought and unrealistic expectation that investing in their child's athletic skills will land them a college scholarship or professional contract someday. These statistics do not lie. It is much more important that investing and coaches spend time helping young kids develop the skills and work ethic needed to survive in "real life" through sports rather than for the purpose of obtaining a scholarship. Dads, this is a reality check. If your goal is to have your child shine solely in the eyes of the sports world, it may end up haunting you and your child in the long run. I say this not to be cautious or negative, but to provide an outlook that many people overlook. Perhaps refocusing and striving to teach your kids to be humble and well-rounded can ensure ultimate success. The game of baseball will also help teach this.

# Making Youth Baseball a Great Experience!

There are keys to making youth baseball a great experience for kids. The roles of coaches, players, and parents are the three main components to a successful Youth League season. Each person needs to act in an appropriate manner and be responsible for his or her actions. Allowing kids to have fun with the game of baseball is important, and when coaches, teammates, and parents come together in a positive way, ALL the kids are sure to have a great Youth League experience. In this section you will learn how, as a parent, you can begin to have a positive impact on your child's baseball development. You will also be pleasantly surprised at how this will improve the quality of your relationship with your child.

The image of a young boy with a mouth stuffed full of bubble gum, a bat and glove laying across the handle bars of his bike as he peddles to the baseball field, reminds us what Youth League baseball is all about. A boy riding his bike, ready and excited to have some real fun, meeting up with his buddies to play a game of baseball, is an iconic vivid memory of our childhood. The excitement of those warm summer days, the thrill of a low-pressure situation where kids can be kids, and the fantasies of making plays or hitting home runs like the big leaguers they see on TV is what drives these kids to the game of baseball.

As coaches and parents, I believe the most important thing that we can do for kids is to realize that when they come to a practice or game–or even playing catch in the back yard–kids want to have fun! Kids want to play with their friends, have a trusted adult presence, and dream of being a big league baseball player. We have a calling in life to help make this possible for every kid. Kids feel cared for when coaches and parents give praise and encouragement. Once players realize that the coach cares, they will effectively buy into the teaching of solid basic baseball skills and give more effort in practice. On top of respect for the kids, if the coaches strategize in a way that the team wins some games–the kids are sure to have fun with you and respect what you have to say to them.

Some coaches feel that yelling and intimidation is the only effective way to get the message across to the players. I teach parents and coaches to gain credibility with their kids by first using direct and clear instruction. Then, when you do raise your voice, make it be of a specific coaching point or of praise to the player. When my voice is raised, it is a clear and direct instruction that creates a sense of intensity. It is never negative or degrading. Challenge yourself to correct a flaw in a player, by first stating a positive. If Caden is constantly struggling to field a backhand ground ball at third base, he will no doubt be frustrated. As a coach you may be tempted to say "Caden, you will be sitting the bench because our team can not have you making these mistakes in the game." This will certainly create a feeling of discouragement in Caden and it will only be a matter of time before he loses interest in the game. Start by saying, "Caden your quickness in reacting to the ball is awesome, now let's finish the play by making sure to keep your glove open and on the ground as you make the back hand play. Let's practice five repetitions of this position before we move on." It is really about how we deliver the message to kids. Let's make sure to encourage by starting with the positive first, correction second, and always finishing with praise and reinforcement.

# Keep it Positive, Fun, and Educational

In this section, use the valuable checklists and questions to ask of a coach, ideal teammate, and for proper behavior of parents in the stands. This will ensure a supportive and educational atmosphere for the young impressionable minds of the Youth Leaguers. These are great reminders for ways that the adults can keep the youth baseball experience positive, fun, and educational. The positive quotes listed throughout this book are great ways to start conversations with your kids, or to provide a positive theme to practices with your players–all while teaching great life lessons through the youth baseball experience.

# Volunteer Coach Guidelines

**BASEBALL CONCEPTS**

**A great Youth League coach for my son Caden would do this:**

## A check list for a coach…

- ☐ Do you set up a pre-season parents' meeting to discuss the season and expectations?

- ☐ Do you bring positive energy as you talk to the kids and prepare them for a practice/game?

- ☐ Are you encouraging and uplifting, filled with positive motives, and can you see in yourself a genuine desire to make it a good experience for the kids?

- ☐ Are you knowledgeable in the game and able to teach the basic baseball skills?

- ☐ Do you ask for other parents to help coach?

- ☐ Can you communicate team policies, practices times, and game changes with the parents?

- ☐ Are you prompt in getting practice started?

- ☐ Do you make practice organized and productive?

- ☐ Have you planned an end-of-the-year party?

## What makes a good volunteer coach?

- ☐ Caring for the kids and makes practice fun for them.

- ☐ Giving high-fives to reward hustle and a good attitude.

- ☐ Placing an arm around the shoulder of a player when correcting or having a teachable moment.

- ☐ Coming to practice organized, and keeps the kids moving with fun drills and a good practice plan.

- ☐ Having patience and a desire to help kids reach their best as people first.

- ☐ Showing the kids how to win without dwelling on the wins and losses.

- ☐ Organizing a team parent meeting prior to the start of the season.

- ☐ Following-through on having an end-of-the-year party that celebrates the kids and the season in a positive way.

# What Makes a Good Teammate?

**A great teammate on any team would do this:**

## A check list for players…

- ☐ Do you bring your glove, bat, batting gloves, and a drink?

- ☐ Do you have a positive attitude? It is the most important tool in your bat bag.

- ☐ Do you help your teammates by encouraging them to practice hard?

- ☐ Are you including everyone? Don't exclude players who are thought to be not as good.

- ☐ Make sure to watch (four) innings of baseball on TV per week. You can learn so much!

- ☐ Do you listen to and respect your coach? You will have many coaches, listen to them all and see how it helps your team.

- ☐ Do you make it a priority to attend all the practices and games?

- ☐ Are you open to playing anywhere? Be flexible in the batting order and at what position you play.

- ☐ Do you make it a point to HAVE FUN?

## What makes a good teammate?

- ☐ Bringing your own equipment or using the teams'. Do not take other player's equipment to use without asking.

- ☐ Refraining from criticizing other players when they make a mistake. Build them up!

- ☐ Leading by example. Let your teammates see that you care about doing things the right way. Hustle, listen to coach, play hard, and do not talk to the umpires or the other team in a poor sportsmanship-like manner.

- ☐ Being HUMBLE. Do not "talk yourself up," nobody wants to play with someone who talks about how good they are. If you're a good player, your teammates will see it by the way you play and how you act.

- ☐ Staying after practice and helping coach pick up the field, bring the equipment to his vehicle, and make sure the dugouts are free from trash and sunflower seeds.

- ☐ Having an attitude of service, think, "What can I do for the team?" Your teammates will think you are pretty cool and will like playing with you.

# Parent Code of Conduct

**BASEBALL CONCEPTS**

## A positive Youth League parent in the stands would act this way:

## A check list for the parents…

- ☐ Are you understanding of the time commitment that the coach is putting in to help the team and your child?

- ☐ Do you avoid talking negatively about the coach and the team to your child?

- ☐ Do you COMMIT to the team?  Have your child at ALL practices and games.  If there is an exception, notify the coach at the start of the season – not a day before.

- ☐ Are you encouraging in the stands and not participating in gossip that can destroy the positive energy of the team, parents, and fans?

- ☐ Do you offer to help the team with tasks such as score keeping, raking the field, or sending email communication.

- ☐ Do you abide by the team policies that the coach sets in place at the start of the season?

- ☐ Do you get your child to practice five minutes early?

- ☐ Are you cordial and tactful when communicating with the coach?

- ☐ Do you avoid shouting at the umpire, the opposing coach, and their fans?

## What makes good little league parents?

- ☐ Being respectful of the team, coach, umpires, opposing team's coaches, players, and fans.

- ☐ Desiring to help the kids learn what good sportsmanship is by modeling it for them.

- ☐ Not being overly obsessed with winning or losing a game!

- ☐ Volunteering their time in a small way such as at the concession stand, field prep, or scheduling for the team or little league program.

- ☐ Coming to the game with a desire to have fun, to enjoy the game, and socialize by building relationships with the other parents.

- ☐ Applauding good plays that the other team makes too.

- ☐ Understanding that this is youth sports, and the kids will imitate what the adults show them – be positive!!

- ☐ Avoiding being prideful in your child's accomplishments.  Be humble!

- ☐ Going easy on your child.  Before, during, and after the game (the car ride home), avoid shouting at your child in a loud voice that may embarrass your child in front of others.  You will look quite silly yourself.

# Developing a "Pre-season Parent Letter"

Communication is the single most important element in leading any type of organization or team. We can prevent or solve most any issue with proper communication. As a coach, your desire is to have a smooth-flowing season without distracting problems. Parents will feel more informed and comfortable if they have good information and communication from the coach; it also gives the coach credibility and initial respect. So if you would like to have your season kicked off in a positive direction where the kids and parents feel that you have your act together, then COMMUNICATE! Below is a sample of how to structure your pre-season introductory parent letter.

### Introduce Yourself:

*(Example)* I am excited to welcome you to another baseball season. My name is coach Jeff VanHuis and I will be your child's baseball coach this year. I have a passion for working with kids and a deep love for the game of baseball, so this season will be a great experience for your child as we teach the game of baseball and what it means to be a good teammate.

### Announce a Parent Meeting:

*(Example)* I have set up a parent meeting for next Thursday night at 6 PM on the baseball field. We will hand out important information pertaining to the start of the season, including a practice schedule, and volunteer sign-up (score keeper, assistant coaching, concession stand workers, drink provider for games/practices). I will also review the coach's contact information and our league's expectations and policies. I will introduce myself to you and also answer any questions you have about the season. I hope at least ONE parent of every child will be present at this meeting.

### Field (Game and Practice) Location:

*State the location of your field. List the typical practice times. Game times are on the schedule.*

### Communication with the Coach:

*(Example)* As the season begins, please contact me via phone or email, or before or after practice with general questions that you my have. After the season is underway, if you have questions regarding playing time, strategy, batting order, or a (non-emergency) situation, I ask that you refrain from discussing it after the game or practice and that you cordially call or email me the following day.

### League Contact Information / Bad Weather Cancellation Plan:

In this section, list any important information that the league has asked you to inform the parents about. If there is a tornado watch or warning, practice and games will be cancelled. If there is inclement weather, please visit our league's website or listen to our local radio station for cancellations.

### Your Vision or Philosophy for The Coming Year:

*(Example)* I have some very valuable knowledge of the game of baseball that I gained while playing college baseball and coaching at various levels. My desire to work with kids is the reason why I coach. I really hope to make this year fun and educational, and for the kids to walk away with some very important life skills. Mr. Smith will also help coach our team this year. He has a passion for kids and is excited to help with our pitchers, and with bookkeeping duties. Together, we desire to have a great season with the kids and teach them how to be their best without over-emphasizing the winning or losing part. We will focus on teaching lessons about preparedness, and striving to be the best team of kids we can be. Parents, you are a key part of the program as well. Please support your child and the team. Please get your player to practices and games on time, since he is a member of the team who has made a commitment to the others. We will strive to make this the most educational baseball season yet–your son will learn some great things this season. I'm looking forward to seeing you at next week's meeting.

"Few men are born brave; many have become so through training and force of discipline."

## WARM-UP AND BODY WORK OUTLINE

What sets a champion apart from the competition is doing the little things better than anyone else. These little things can be developed all year long and it starts with a player's body. If the body is not conditioned (even as a thirteen year-old boy) the maximum potential of the player will be restricted. I do not support intense weight training for kids thirteen years old and younger, as their bodies need to be developed first. I do, however, recommend body work conditioning, even if it is very light. If nothing else, this starts to create a sense of work ethic and an attitude of understanding the total process of what it takes to be successful in sport and life. I encourage my players to be sure they are working harder than anyone else, and that becomes our focus.

# Give 100% Effort

**"Remember, you meet your opponents, not their reputation."**

All young ball players dream of hitting home runs, pitching no-hitters, and making a diving catch on the field. However, it is important to remember these all-star highlights are the end result of that player putting in many hours of practice and training all year long. Far too often, young kids watch sports highlight reels and wish they had the skills needed to make those jaw-dropping plays. The secret is that with fierce discipline and determination these skills may be theirs too! Players at all levels just need to be taught how to put in the time and strive to be the best they can absolutely be. By letting that be the driving factor, and by watching how the adults in their lives model this work ethic, everything else will fall in to place. It is all about a process.

A baseball player's greatest physical strength is to have a healthy and strong core muscle group, as this will provide him with endurance to pitch late in games and have proper rotation to obtain maximum velocity, as well as to have a strong core rotation as he hits or throws a ball in general. Baseball is a sport that requires specific core muscle and cardiovascular strengthening. Lifting weights and distance running are certainly good conditioning, but baseball players need a specific concentrated workout we call a rotational warm up. The movements of the baseball player are circular, vertical, and linear, thus the reason for these baseball specific warm-ups and muscle-building exercises. The exercises outlined in this section are designed to assist the baseball player strengthen the core muscle groups such as the abs and lower back areas. These muscle groups work together in a player's body as rotation occurs in throwing or hitting the ball.

This warm up and body work routine is to be used before every practice and game during the season, and three times per week during the off season training time. I have personally witnessed a drastic reduction in the amount of arm soreness from my players as a result of using this rotational warm-up vs. the traditional stretching methods that coaches have used for years. Muscle groups tend to be cold at the beginning of practice, and stretching those muscles can be ineffective. Our players certainly feel the difference and are ready to perform once the rotational warm up is complete and blood has had a chance to circulate through the tendons and muscles during the routine.

Champions are made when no one is watching! If a player gives a 100% all the time, they will eventually face someone who has not and they will win every time. Help your player develop this type of mental toughness and help them make this the goal each time they work out. The bodywork activities are something that we do after every baseball work out or practice. Coaches may want to choose a couple to work on each day and mix it up often to keep it as exciting as possible for the players. These bodywork techniques are very easy to do, and can be performed anywhere. I teach my kids to spend fifteen minutes each day doing their body work exercise before they shower.  If a player commits to working on these exercises there will be a significant difference in his core strength. After all, being a successful baseball player is not just showing up on game day and expecting to perform. It is the many hours spent behind closed doors working as hard as you possibly can to prepare your body to play baseball. Nothing great or worthwhile is going to come easily, there has to be a will to work for it!

**"Baseball is more than a game to American children...For over 150 years, baseball has helped teach us about adversity and courage, success and failure, disappointment and hope." – Kenesaw Mountain Landis**

# Rotational Warm-Up

1. **Focus: Lower Half of Body**

    A.  <u>Knees tight together</u>- Bend knees and push in on the outside of the knees with hands.  Very quickly move knees/legs in the following routines: Side/Side, Back/Forth, Circles Left/Right, Figure 8, *(ten reps of each).*

    B.  <u>Feet spread wide</u>- Bend at the waist and knees and have elbows firmly against the inside of knees with hands together in the prayer position.  Keep the butt low and back straight.  *Follow the routines as above.*

    C.  <u>Knee Bends</u>- Place your feet in position, with hands on hips, and bend at the knees, (five bends of each).  Positions: Normal, Duck Feet, and Pigeon-Toed.

2. **Focus: Upper Half of Body**

    A.  <u>Trunk Twists</u>- Hands/arms up and rotate 180 degrees back/forth.  Keep the head still facing forward with eyes fixed and focused straight ahead.

(fifteen reps)

    B.  <u>Forearms and Shoulders</u>- Clasp hands together with the thumb up and thumb down, apply pressure by PULLING hands/fingers against one another.  Quickly, move arms/shoulders in the following routines: side/side, forward/back, swim forward/back (ten reps of each).

    C.  <u>Forearms and Shoulders</u>- SAME AS (B) ABOVE, except instead of pulling, apply pressure by PUSHING against hands/fingers (ten reps of each).

    D.  <u>Arms Up and Out, Even with Shoulders</u>-  Technique: ***Position 1-*** Lift the arms up so that the hands and elbows are level at shoulder height.  Point hands straight out from the body and keep them **flat** facing the ground.  The elbows should have a 90-degree bend, so that fingers point forward. Move hands and arms, while rotating the shoulders in the following routines: small circle forward, big circle forward, small circle backwards, big circle backwards, swim arms forward and backwards (ten reps of each).  *This will burn, players will get tired, but  they need to fight and work through it.*  **Position 2** – Same technique as Position 1, except that palms of hands face out with thumbs down,  (ten reps of each routine). **Position 3** – Same technique as Position 1, except that the palms of hands face inward with thumbs up (ten reps of each routine).

Position 1

Position 2

Position 3

3. **Focus: Cardiovascular Warm Up** *(pick three of these to run before a practice or game)*

    A. All running should be done in the outfield grass, start on the foul line and run until even with second base.

Jog down, jog backwards back
Skip down, skip backwards back
Karaoke down and back

Karaoke

High knees down, high knees back
Scissors down, Scissors back *(Stride by hopping up, separating legs in the air while pumping arms – form running)*
Sprint down 70%, walk back
Sprint down 100%, walk back

4. **You may now have the players begin throwing to "loosen up" their arms.**

# Body Work

> **"Men are not prisoners of fate, but only prisoners of their own minds."**

1. **Body Work**

   A. <u>Leg lifts</u>: Sit on the ground, lean back onto the elbows, have glove pinched between the knees and bring knees up to nose. For each rep, the legs should go from the ground to the nose. (twenty-five reps).

   B. <u>Bridge holds (Prones)</u>: Push up position, except that the forearms are flat to the ground. Hold the body in a straight position for one to two minutes for a youth player, working up to five minutes (two reps).

   C. <u>Supermans</u>: Lay on the stomach and lift the arms and legs up as high as possible, and hold for as long as possible (five reps).

D.  Walking lunges: Players take a long stride, bend the front knee and keep it over the front toe.  Be sure to keep the back knee 1" off the ground (thirty reps).

E.  Pick Pockets: Sit on the ground, cross legs and lift them slightly off the ground. With both hands gripping a glove, move hands quickly back and forth from hip to hip (fifty reps).

F.  Pulse 5:  Do five push-ups and on the fifth one hold in the down position for five seconds, then repeat (four reps initially, but work to increase reps).

2.  **Cool Down** *To be done After Practice or Baseball Workout*
    A.  Pitchers who throw more than three (3) innings are to jog around the warning track for 15-20 minutes after the game or practice.  This is done to work out the lactic acid build up in the elbow and shoulder joints.  No Ice!

    B.  Avoid stretching the tendons of the arm, only stretch specific muscle groups that need to be addressed.  If the arm is sore, perform the "upper body focus" of the rotational warm-up and run for 15-20 minutes after a throwing session.

    C.  The best way to strengthen your arm is proper off-season throwing and long toss!

"Whether you think you can or think you can't – you're right!"

## DRILLS and TECHNIQUES

In baseball, a **five-tool player** is one who excels at hitting for average, hitting for power, base-running skills and speed, throwing ability, and fielding abilities. For most of his career, Ken Griffey Jr. was considered a five-tool player. The best way to achieve these skills as a young kid is to be a well-rounded player. Players should avoid identifying themselves as only a shortstop and a home run hitter. Players should spend ample time focusing on all the facets of the game. There are so many skill areas within the game of baseball and these skills take years to develop. Using the proper skills and techniques will certainly give each young player an opportunity to become a five tool player, and along the way learning a valuable work ethic in becoming what they want to be!

# Doing Things the Right Way

> "The key to success is to climb the ladder instead of waiting for the elevator."

A past article in the USA Today asked, and then did some follow up research on, the question: "What is the MOST difficult skill to perform in all of sports?" The conclusion was that hitting a round shaped baseball traveling at 80+mph with a round shaped bat is the single most difficult task in sports today. An athletic body with decent build, quickness, and competitive mindset are just the beginnings of a good baseball player. However these attributes alone will not develop a super-star baseball player. Our sport is one that requires many different skill-specific details to make a complete player.

Three months prior to the start of each season, I spend two days per week working with my players in the specific areas of hitting, pitching, and fielding. These skill areas need to develop over time and cannot be achieved without constant repetition over a long period. I have seen the most athletic, strong, and quick athletes struggle to field a ground ball or fail to hit a baseball consistently, this occurs simply because not enough proper repetition has been practiced. The key to this, however, is to practice the correct technique early on in a young player's development. Each child's body moves and works in a different way, and kids will adapt to what works best for them. Usually, the way kids discover technique is by watching professional players on TV or other kids in their Youth League. Often times these techniques are not correct for the player and the child continues to practice repetitiously the incorrect technique, which is the single biggest detriment to a player's skill development. It takes one thousand correct repetitions of a skill technique to offset one bad habit! This is why it is essential to provide your player with the correct skills, drills, and techniques as early as possible in their developmental years.

I recommend working through the skill and drill techniques over the course of a three to four week period, and focus only on one or two skills at a time to avoid overwhelming the young player. Once the skill is mastered, then you can move on to teaching the next skill and repeating the process until all the skill areas are covered. Baseball agility and fluidity in skill quickness is the most desirable attribute to develop in your player.

Never overlook the most important tool in a player's bat bag: their attitude. It all starts there. A poor attitude is like a cancer that spreads throughout the body, eventually consuming the natural skills of the players. When this consumes the player, it passes to others on the team and the downward spiral is inevitable. Start practice by teaching kids what you expect in the attitude department. For example: never look at or back talk to an umpire, and when a player strikes out they are to run back to the dugout–not walk. Players are never to appear lazy or just going through the motions. Coaches and parents, you need to have consequences in place for when this occurs. One could argue that this is just boys being boys. On one level this may be true, but our society needs these boys to become men. When they are forty years old and raising a family, we need their attitude to be mature, polite, hardworking, and appropriate. If kids do not have this instilled in them at a young age, it is very tough to change later on in their life. Parents, step up to the plate and take charge in your kids' lives, do not let them walk all over you and react by saying that they are just being kids.

**BASEBALL CONCEPTS**

Baseball Concepts' tips for making a difference in each age group in youth baseball. If you are a parent looking to work with your child at home or a coach working with a full team, these tips will help you. Your child and team will enjoy playing baseball with you if practice is active, fun, and educational.

## Coaching Tips          "Remember that winners do what losers don't want to."

### Ages 4-7

**1. Fear of the Ball.** Kids at this age need to be comfortable with catching the ball. Start out by using a tennis ball to play catch with to reduce the initial fear of the ball.

**2. Attention Span.** Kids will need to be busy at practice or in the back yard. Playing catch, hitting, base running, fielding, and scrimmaging all should be done in ten-minute increments. This will also create a productive practice hour.

**3. Hitting off the Tee.** Have a bucket of balls (fifteen) next to the tee and keep placing balls on the tee as the player hits, picking the balls up once the bucket is empty. This will keep them focused and aid with their short attention span. Keep all the other kids clear from the area where bats are swinging and be sure they wear a helmet.

### Ages 8-12

**1. Teach the Basics.** Kids at this age are really starting to take an interest in learning the game. Keep it simple; try teaching 2-3 skills per week and focusing on those until the player is ready to move on.

**2. Pitching.** At this age, have players learn pitching from the stretch position. It is easier for them vs. from the wind-up. Stick to throwing a two-seam or four-seam fastball until the player develops.

**3. Hitting.** Pitch overhand to the player from behind an L-screen that is 15' feet away. Give ten pitches and then a rest to avoid fatigue in the player. The coach can also sit on a bucket and throw overhand batting practice from behind the L-screen, this will give the kids a good perspective.

### Ages 13-18

1. **Playing Catch.** Players can strengthen their arms and develop "quick" hands by playing short and long toss catch. This should be done 3-4 times per week for fifteen minutes each time.

**2. Body Work.** At this age the strength of the body becomes a factor. Proper weight training and core body work is essential to the player's baseball development. Body work should be performed 3-4 times per week in the offseason.

**3. Hitting off a Tee.** Players at this level can benefit from tee work. Incorporate this into every batting practice and be sure proper technique is being used. Rotate between tee work, soft toss, and the live cage for a well-rounded batting practice.

# Coaching "The Little Things"

## 1.    Scouting the Opponent

Instruct your players to stand just outside the dugout in a single file line as your team watches the other team warm up and take their pre-game fielding practice.  This can also be an intimidating presence for the opposing team to experience.  Watch for opposing player's strengths and weaknesses making sure your players refrain from speaking any loud un-sportsman like comments as they watch the other team play.

## 2.    Taking the Field

A.    Players should sprint hard to their positions on the field in under ten seconds.

B.    First baseman and Centerfielder should ALWAYS have a practice ball in their glove as they take the field.
     i.    These positions lead the pre-inning warm-ups.
     ii.    Designate a substitute player as the pre-inning catcher to warm-up the pitcher.
     (Use in situations when current game catcher puts on his gear following an at-bat).

C.    When an offensive teammate makes the final out of an inning and remains on the field ready to now play defense, have a player bring the glove and hat to this player.  This helps the game move along at a good pace.

## 3.    In-game player responsibilities

A.    On deck batter for plays-at-the-plate
     - Tell base runner to stay up or slide into the plate

B.    On deck batter for foul balls to the back stop
     - After play is dead, assist the umpire in speeding up the game by retrieving the ball and giving it back to the home plate ump.

## 4.    Attitude

A.    Tell players never to look at or say anything to an umpire after a questionable call is made against them.

B.    Insist hustle, positive attitude, doing things the correct way, and giving 100% for the time that they are on the field.

C.    Encourage players to talk and chatter.  During each inning (on offense and defense), players are to shout positive encouragements to their teammates.  This creates an atmosphere that caters to motivation and teamwork – which is essential for every successful team to possess.

# Catching Drills and Techniques

## 1. Proper Stance: Signal Stance, Receiving Stance, Man on Stance

A. Signal Stance

- ❑ The catcher's butt is low and sitting on the heels.
- ❑ The catcher's feet are close together and knees pointed at pitcher.
- ❑ The catcher's chest is straight with chin up and the elbow of the bare hand resting against the hip. The wrist of the glove hand rests on the knee with fingers pointed down to shield the sign being given.

B. Receiving Stance (no man on)

- ❑ Have toes pointed out slightly towards first and third bases, heels kicked out, butt low to the ground.
- ❑ Open the glove, hold the glove arm with a slight bend in it.
- ❑ Center your chest on the middle of the plate (provide the pitcher with a big target).
- ❑ Swing your body to catch the ball (see receiving).

C. Receiving Stance (man on)

- ❑ Have toes pointed out towards first and third bases with heels kicked out and butt off your heels.
- ❑ Open the glove, glove arm slightly bent, bare hand with a fist behind glove or behind leg.
- ❑ Swing your body to catch the ball on throwing side of the body.

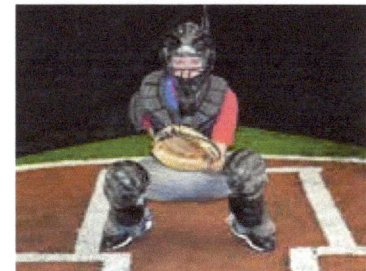

_DRILL PRACTICE:_ _Work the stances in partners- help each other out, tell them what they are doing._

## 2. Receiving & Framing

A. Relaxed Stance.

B. Receive ball in front.

C. Relax your wrist- slight turn as pitcher gets ready to release ball.

D. Frame with the wrist, not with arm.

E. Swing the body to receive ball in the center of your body.

F. Framing:

- Arm has a slight bend, not stiff as a board.
- Fingers always point back to the pitcher when catching the ball
- Don't frame a ball that is not close to the zone.
- Drop knee technique for low and away

### DRILL PRACTICE:

**Bare hand framing:** *Two Catchers (each have a ball) 10 -12 ft apart in the receiving stance. Toss the ball for other catcher to receive with their bare hand. Receiving catcher focuses on relaxed arm swinging body to side of the plate that the ball is on, and fingers pointing back to pitcher (ten reps).*

Partner Feed  Use Bare Hand

**Framing with glove:** *one catcher receives throws and works on framing, while the other catcher does the same or works on receiving with a man on (ten reps).*

Use Glove

## 3. Blocking the Pitch

A. Comfortable stance with butt off the heels (protecting against pass ball).
B. Drive knees & shoulders down into the ground.
C. Smother the ball.
D. Bare hand behind glove.
E. Push with feet to get outside to block pitches off the plate.

### DRILL PRACTICE:

**The Gauntlet:** with balls placed randomly on the ground, the catcher proceeds through blocking each one and hopping back up and in front of the next one.

The Gauntlet

**Three ball blocking:** One ball in front and one to each side. One catcher points and the other catcher goes down to block it. Focus on driving knees and shoulders down and pushing off on the feet to get outside to block outside pitches. Run drill very quickly. React to partner as he points out the next ball.

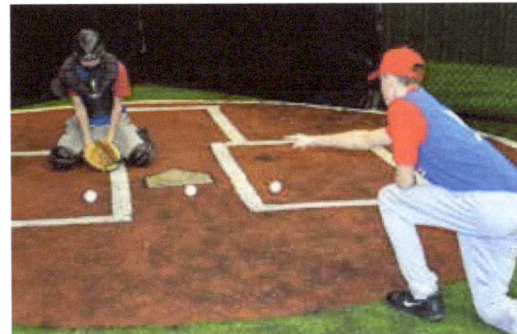

Three Ball Blocking

**Throwing balls in the dirt:** Rapid fire- throw the ball straight at catcher wearing gear, then off to the sides. Catcher is to block the balls as quickly as he can. Partner is to have ten balls in his glove or nearby to keep the drill moving. *(Note: there is no photo of this drill)*

## 4. Blocking the Plate on a "Play at the Plate"

A. Heels on the plate, do not straddle.
B. Bend the knees, ready to receive the ball from the fielder.
C. Catch with two hands holding the ball with bare hand in the glove.
D. Drop the right knee to block the plate from the runner.
E. Tag with the back of the glove.
F. Recover and look for further plays.

**_DRILL PRACTICE:_** Find the plate, and then receive the ball, brace for impact!! Throw the ball to the catcher as he works on technique, (fifteen reps).

## 5. Footwork and Throwing

A. Glove to hand transfers.
B. Short (punchy) throwing motion right from the ear.
C. Quick feet = quick release = quick throw.
D. Square to the target, push with the feet, rotate hips, and follow through.

**_DRILL PRACTICE:_** *"Pop Time" with a partner.* In the stance, receive ball and then work on a quick transfer and good foot work, staying low and pushing off with the back foot. Throw ball down to second base. Each time work on quickness and accuracy, (eight reps).

**_Fast Fact:_** A quick pop time for a high school player is 1.8-2.3 seconds. That is the time from when the catch is received from the pitcher to the ball's arrival at second base.

# Infield Drills and Techniques

## 1. Proper Fielding Stance and "Ready" Position

Feet are shoulder width apart with a slight flex in the knees, glove held out front and open. Be ready to react when the pitched ball enters the hitting zone!
***DRILL PRACTICE:*** *practice the stance and getting into the "ready" position.*

## 2. Fielding a Ground Ball

**With Glove**

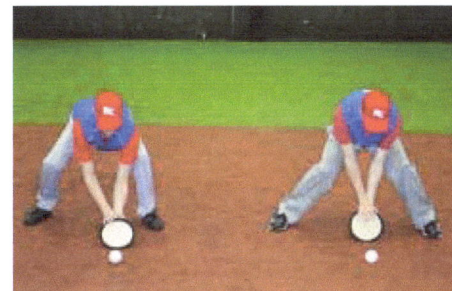

**Drill Practice Variation: Use a paddle**

A. Always move forward, charge the ball. 1-2-3 approach to fielding the ball: (1) right foot, (2) left foot, (3) bend at knees and extend arms to ball.
B. Keep thumb to thumb contact while both hands are extended out to the ground ball, always use two hands and field the ball centered in front.
C. Feet are wider than shoulders, bend at the knees, butt down, two hands extended, thumb to thumb, fielding ball out front. Soft hands in receiving, then pull the ball securely into the stomach.

***DRILL PRACTICE:*** *Practice the 1-2-3 approach without a ball, and then practice with a ball being rolled 15' away. Then hit ground balls to players at 90' away, (fifteen reps each).*

*Variation - Ground Ball Drill:* Have the players start by sitting on the ground. As the coach hits the ball, player must get up and quickly and correctly field the ball.

This is a fun twist to the drill that will keep your players engaged and having fun with fielding ground balls.

*Coaches can turn this in to a "fun" team competition!*

**DRILL PRACTICE:** *"Shuffle Drill" for proper infielding technique and to build strength in the legs.*

A.   Practice in partners: This drill is to be done without a glove. The fielding player begins the drill 10' from partner and is in the proper fielding position.

B.   A ball is rolled 10' to the right, fielding player remains in the fielding position. Staying low, he shuffles to the ball and fields it.

C.   Fielding player then underhand tosses the ball back to partner.

D.   Ball is then rolled 10' to the left, and the player shuffles over to the left to field the ball.

E.   Repeat this sequence, back and forth, fifteen reps and then switch with partner.

(B) Roll ball to the right

(C) Underhand toss

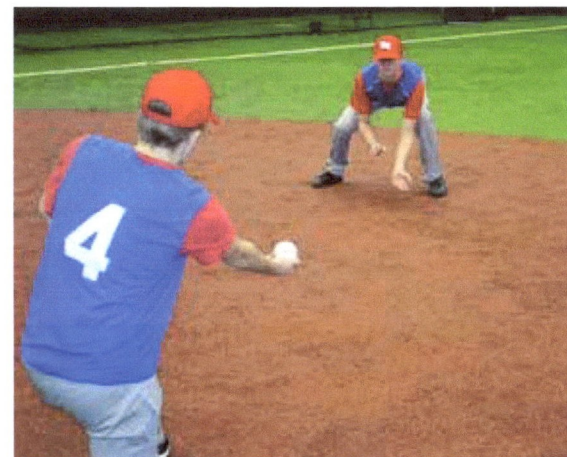

(D) Roll ball to the left

## 3. Short Hops:

  A. Assuming a normal fielding stance, player brings his glove hand to the ground and top hand thumb to thumb. Keep the glove low to the ground and come up with the ball.
  B. Assuming the backhand stance (righty), the glove is on the ground with the weight-bearing leg behind his glove. Keep the glove low to the ground and come up to the ball.
  C. Assuming the glove side stance in the athletic position, bring the glove to the ground and field with one hand. Keep glove low to the ground and come up to the ball.

(A)                              (B)                              (C)

***DRILL PRACTICE:*** *A coach or another player (standing 15' away) throws ball rapidly so it lands 3' in front of the player, creating a "short hop". Player reacts by bringing his glove up as he fields the ball. Practice all three stances, ten reps).*

## 4. Throwing the Ball:

Step towards target

Accurate Throw

  A. After the ball is fielded, bring the right foot over the left foot while pushing off the right foot to throw. Step into the throw!
  B. The ball is brought up in a quick motion to behind the ear and thrown directly toward target; player then follows the throw. The ball transfer from the glove to throwing position must be short and quick, not long like and outfielder or pitcher.
  C. Be sure players follow their throw to the target by taking two or three strides towards target after releasing the ball.

***DRILL PRACTICE:*** *step towards target with right foot over left foot, bringing the ball to the ear and throwing to the target. Follow the throw by taking three or four strides towards target (eight reps of live ground balls).*

## 5. Starting a double play: (DP)

**SS and 2B:** Charge the ball, field the ball, and in one quick motion give a strong throw to second base.

**SS and 2B**: When fielding the ball close to the bag, give a strong underhand *"FEED"* to the base and follow your feed with a few steps towards the base.

**2B:** When fielding the ball deep in the hole, second baseman will re-position himself quickly (either by spinning around or by a jump pivot) to give a solid throw to the base.

**SS:** When fielding the ball deep in the hole, SS will plant his right foot and then give a strong, fluid, accurate throw to second base.

**SS and 2B:** Fielder's primary job is to get the out at second, think about nothing else until this occurs or the play breaks down.

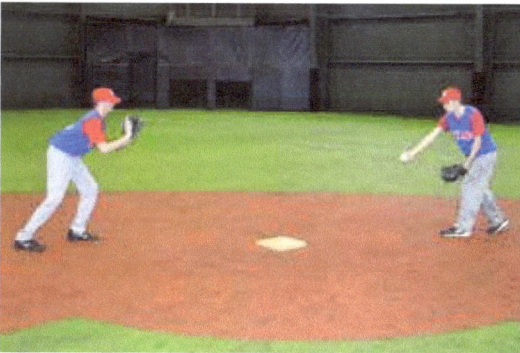

| Underhand feed | Second baseman pivots square to the base | SS in the hole, fluid toss to the base |

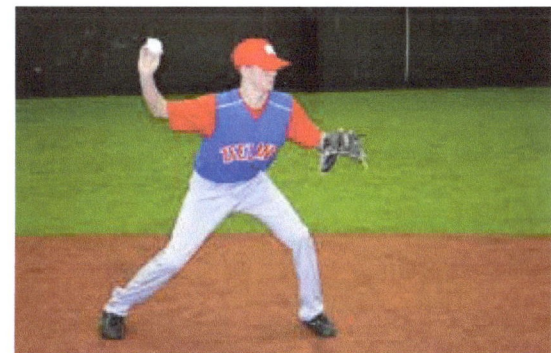

## Double Play Tip:

Important: be sure to get the out at second base first. Do not be distracted by the base runners. Focus on what can be controlled and making a good execution of the play. A common mistake is made when the fielder is rushing while making the play. Just remember to practice many repetitions of being as focused as possible and the quickness will come with the more reps that are taken.

# 6. Turning a Double Play:

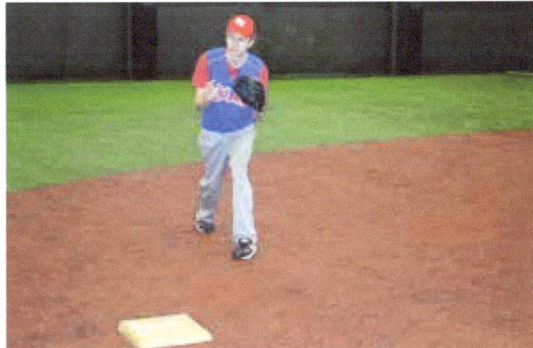

**A.** ***Second baseman receiving ball*** at the bag: get in line with the ball and prepare to receive the ball.  Do not wait at the base.  Time it so that you catch the ball, then step on second base with your left foot, cross over the bag, plant and throw <u>accurately</u> to first.

**B.** ***Short Stop receiving ball*** at the bag: Get in line with the back corner of the bag and the ball, do not wait at the base, time it, catch the ball first, then clip the back corner of the base with right foot, clear the base path and give a strong <u>accurate</u> throw to first base.

***<u>DRILL PRACTICE:</u>*** *double plays in partners:*
Roll grounder (20' away)
Hit ground balls (60' away)
Hit ground balls (full distance)

31

# Outfield Techniques and Drills

## 1. Proper Outfielding Stance:

    A.  Feet are shoulder width apart, knees are bent, and glove is held out front and open – be ready to react when the pitched ball enters the hitting zone.

    B.  Fly ball hit at you: first step is back, read the ball, stay behind it while getting into position to catch the ball.

    C.  Fly ball hit over head: sprint back quickly while tracking the baseball over your shoulder. Be sure to run on the balls of your feet to eliminate head movement from pounding feet. The catch will be made in stride and over the shoulder.

*DRILL PRACTICE:* *practice each stance and react (without a ball) to each scenario, then react with a softly thrown or batted ball, (ten reps).*

        (A)        (B)        (C)

## 2. Tracking the Ball:

    A.  Fly ball hit to the player's left or right side: take a direct path to where the ball will land. Beat the ball to the spot, set feet while staying behind the ball as the catch is made. Important: Take a direct path to ball, predict where the ball will land and sprint to that spot!

Players point to where the ball will land  Take a straight path to ball

*DRILL PRACTICE:* *Player's stand in a group in Center Field. Coach throws a ball far to the left - instruct players to point to where they think the ball will land. Repeat by throwing a ball to the right side as well, (six reps). Next, have players react by running on a* <u>straight line</u> *to the spot and catch the ball! Run drill by either throwing or hitting a fly ball.*

### 3. Catching the Ball

Call the ball <u>loudly</u>, "I got it, I got it".
  A.  Run to the spot where the ball will come down.
  B.  Stay behind the baseball, feet set in athletic position, and two hands out reaching up to ball.
  ***DRILL PRACTICE:*** *throw or hit a fly ball and have each player practice the technique, (five reps).*

### 4. Catching a Ball "TAG UP"

  A.  Be sure to stay 2 steps behind the ball, bring your momentum forward to and through the ball as the catch is made. If runner tags, throw through to base.
  ***DRILL PRACTICE:*** *throw or hit a fly ball and have each player practice the technique, (five reps).*

### 5. "Tweeners" and Fly Ball Communication

  A.  Ball hit between two outfielders: Center fielder is in charge and has the right to "call off" the corner outfielder as they converge on a ball hit between them.
  B.  A pop-up between the outfielder and infielder: The outfielder has the right to "call off" the infielder as they converge on the ball hit between them.

Call It!

  ***DRILL PRACTICE:*** *Set up players in two groups, designate a CF position, and then softly throw or hit a ball directly between the players. Players are to call the ball loudly before the catch is made, (fifteen reps).*

## 6. Crow Hops w/ Throw

Field Grounder →    Crow Hop →

A.   Hit/throw ground ball to outfielder; as the player quickly charges the baseball, he fields the ball on the glove side of his body.  Player then jumps up and "crow hops" a throw.  A "crow hop" is used to initiate powerful forward momentum into the throw.

***DRILL PRACTICE:***  *Hit ground ball (or in the air) to outfielder, player will field ball and "crow hop" a throw to target, (five reps).*

## 7. Over the Shoulder Catches

Throwing Shoulder →    Glove Side →

A.   Have players get into a single file line.  Have players run straight away from the line, while looking over their glove shoulder.  A ball is tossed high and deep as player tracks the ball down (in stride) makes the catch over his glove shoulder.

***DRILL PRACTICE:***  *Repeat this drill looking over the throwing shoulder as well.  Each player should get five reps over each shoulder.*

## 8. Hitting the Cut-Off Man

INF Cut-off →

A.   After the outfielder catches the ball, he looks and finds the "cut-off man" (infielder) and delivers a solid throw to his chest.

B.   Outfielder is looking and listening for the infielder who has his hands high in the air and is yelling, "Cut, cut, cut."

***DRILL PRACTICE:***  *In partners: practice catching a fly ball, then finding the cut-off man and giving a strong throw to the chest.  This needs to be done quickly and effectively, (five reps).*

# Hitting Techniques and Drills

**BASEBALL CONCEPTS**

Rhythm, Load, Stride, Lead with Hands, and Explode!

## 1. Proper Stance: (Rhythm)

    A. Feet are shoulder width apart, slight flex in the knees, hands are on the bat and held slightly above the back shoulder, eyes are fixed on the pitcher.

    B. Player should have some rhythm in the stance to assist in timing the ball and to also assist in getting him into the hitting position.

    C. Weight is 40% on front leg and 60% back leg.

**_DRILL PRACTICE:_** _In front of a mirror, get into the position and evaluate the technique. Be sure to practice body rhythm, (eight reps)._

## 2. Load:

    A. As pitch is being released, load: shift hands slightly back and rotate your weight to 70% on the back leg – this gets the hitter in the hitting position.

**_DRILLPRACTICE:_** _Without a thrown ball: practice loading, shifting hands and distributing weight to get into the hitting position, (eight reps)._

## 3. Stride:

    A. Lift up the front foot and stride straight toward the pitcher 3-6". This is to initiate forward momentum in the swing.

**_DRILL PRACTICE:_** _With and without a thrown ball: the stride technique, (8 reps)._

1. Proper Stance

Hands Back

2. Load

Keep head still and level

Lift Foot

3. Stride

## 4. The Swing: (Lead with Hands)

A. Begin the swing coming from the load position by bringing the hands forward and down towards the hitting zone.

B. Hands should be brought into the hitting zone, as player begins slight rotation in the hips – do not pull out the front shoulder until contact with the ball is made – lead with hands.

    i. **Explode:** As bat and ball contact is made, rotate hips, keeping front leg straight and pivoting on the back foot.

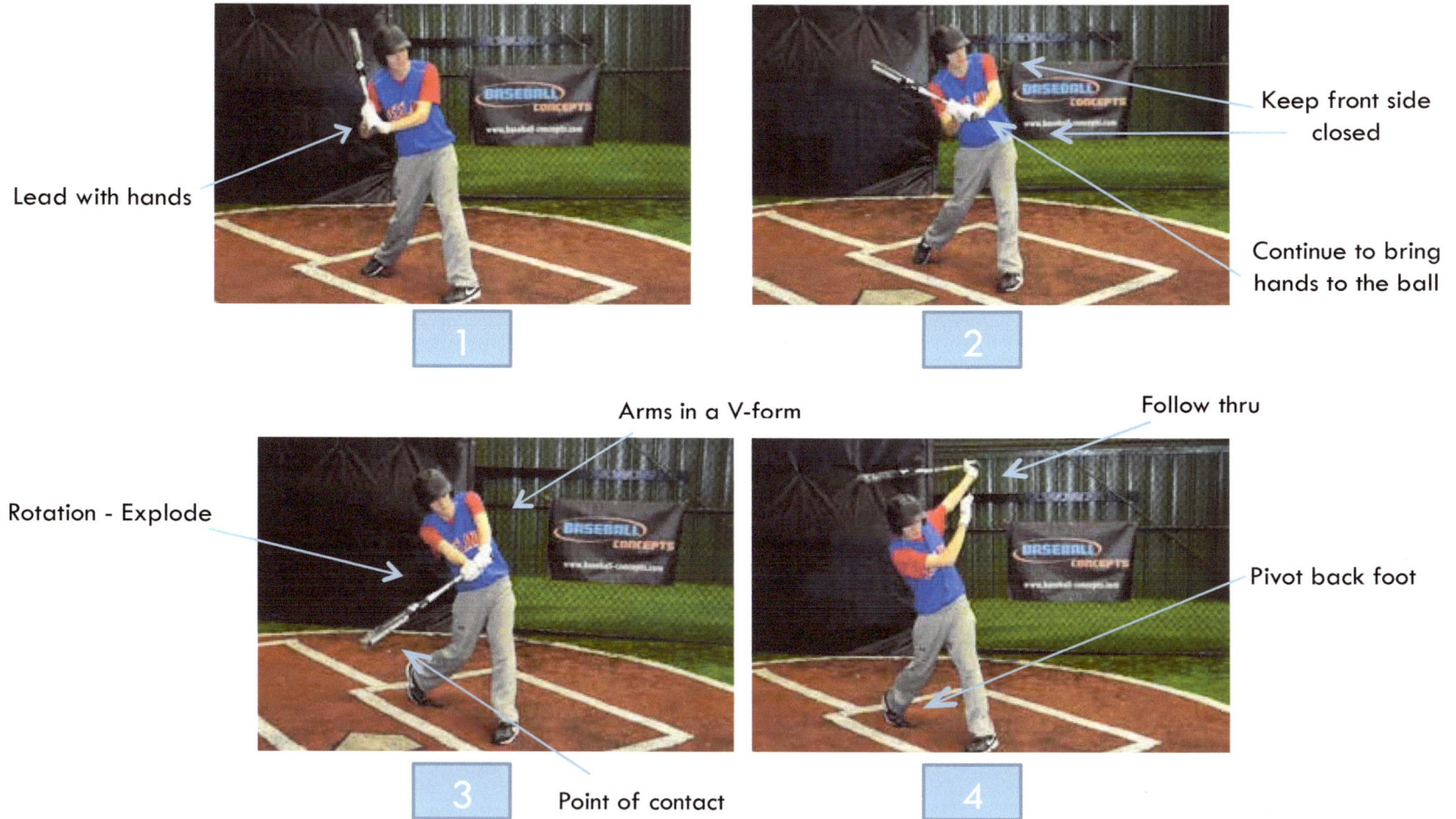

Lead with hands

1

Keep front side closed

Continue to bring hands to the ball

2

Arms in a V-form

Begin Hip Rotation - Explode

3

Point of contact

Follow thru

Pivot back foot

4

***DRILL PRACTICE:*** *In partners:* <u>soft toss</u> *a ball to the hitter.* <u>T-Drill,</u> *working on the swing with a stationary ball on a tee.*

**A. Soft Toss Drills:** partner will sit on a bucket 6' away. Be sure ball feeder is back from the hitter and clear from the swing, (eight reps per player).
  i. Underhand toss the ball into the hitting zone.
  ii. Hitter takes a full swing at the ball driving it into a sock net.
  iii. Proper stance, load, stride, and swing explosion.
  iv. Be sure to the give hitter time to get set into his stance before tossing the next ball.
  ***Variation:*** Underhand tosses can be delivered from behind the hitter as well, just another version of the drill.
       Soft toss can be done with or without the stride.

| Normal Soft Toss | From Behind Soft Toss | Hitter drives ball into net |

**B. T-Drills:** (eight reps of each drill per player)
  i. <u>**Top Half:**</u> Square up lower half of the body to the sock-net, then rotate top half so that it is square with the Tee. Hitter then takes a full swing (with top half only), and just after contact with the ball, he rolls his wrists so to not move or pull away with the front shoulder. Goal is to drive ball straight into the net while keeping the front side of the body closed.
  ii. <u>**Small bat:**</u> Hold with the bottom hand. With the top hand, grab the front shoulder. Practice a full swing while driving the bottom hand to the baseball and keeping the front side closed.
  iii. <u>**Full swing:**</u> Player works the entire swing: Rhythm, Load, Stride, Lead with the hands, explode while rotating the hips! This can be done with a regular bat or with a thin barrel training bat (shown in picture).

Training Bat

| Top Half | Small Bat Start | Small Bat Finish | Full Swing |

## 5. Bunting:

    A.    Stance:
- i. Get squared up to the pitcher by pivoting with the feet so that shoulders are square. The hitter must keep his feet in the box while bunting the ball.
- ii. Keep slight flex in the knees.
- iii. Keep bat barrel in the hitting zone.

    B.    Hands:
- i. Keep the bottom hand near the knob of the bat, slide the top hand up to just below the barrel of the bat.
- ii. Do not wrap the top hand around the bat.
- iii. Keep barrel of the bat slightly up; hands should be lower. DON'T tip the barrel down to bunt a low pitch.

    C.    The bunt:
- i. As the ball enters the hitting zone, catch the ball with the barrel and direct ball to the ground. Remember: Keep the barrel of the bat up.
- ii. If the pitch is lower in the zone, bend with knees to bunt it vs. lowering the barrel of the bat (a pop-up will result).

    D.    Squeeze Bunt
- i. As the pitcher begins his delivery to the plate, the base runner at third breaks for home as a straight steal.
- ii. Hitter lays down a bunt and gets out of the way of the runner as soon as possible.

**_DRILL PRACTICE:_** _in partners, stand 15' away and throw to each other, practice proper bunting techniques and bunting the ball on the ground. This can also be practiced from a pitching machine or live from full mound to plate distance._

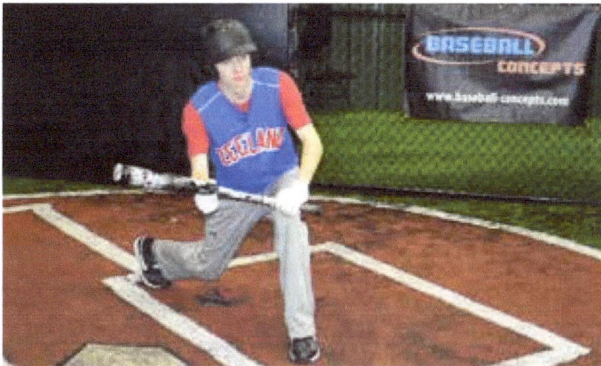

(A) Stance

(B) Hands

# Pitching Techniques and Drills

## 1. Technique from the Stretch

    A.  Put back foot on the rubber, lean in to get the sign, check the base runners, and then come to the set position.

    B.  Check the runner, refocus eyes on the catcher's glove, pump your knee and pitch the ball to the plate.

    C.  Pump the knee, get to the Equal and Opposite position by driving hip towards the plate. Upon dropping the hand with ball out of the glove, your thumb travels next to the thigh, then to the sky, through the slot and down across the other side.

    D.  Follow through after the pitch is thrown.

| Get the sign | Check Runner | Pump Knee | Equal/Opposite | Chin Over knee |

## 2. Technique from the Wind-Up

    A.  Begin with both feet on the rubber, square to the plate. Glove up, throwing hand at your side. Look in for the sign.

    B.  Bring the throwing hand up and into the glove to grip the ball.

    C.  For a right hander, step back with your left foot, bring the right foot to the front edge of rubber, pump knee, and deliver pitch to the plate.

    D.  Upon dropping the hand with ball out of the glove, your thumb travels next to the thigh, then to the sky, through the slot and down across the other side.

    E.  Follow through after the pitch is thrown.

| Get the Sign | Step Back | Follow Through |

**3.** <u>**Towel Drills** *Practice*</u>**:** *In partners, obtain a dish towel and use these drills to hone the pitching mechanics in a very effective and arm safe way that will instill muscle memory for the developing pitcher.*

A. <u>Square up and have glove in front:</u> Partner will stand 5' away (facing chest to chest) with the glove held out and at waist height. Assume the athletic position, feet slightly wider than shoulders, flex the knees, glove hand up and in front at chest height, with throwing hand griping the towel bring together inside the glove. Maintain this position while executing the drill. Bring throwing hand/towel around in a quick throwing motion snapping the towel on partners hand. Remember to hold glove firmly in front of chest, no hip rotation, just arm slot action.

Arm Slot Action  The Finish

B. <u>Equal and Opposite:</u> Same position as previous. But now as the player reaches back with throwing hand/towel, he also reaches to partner with the palm of his glove, and as he brings the towel around in a quick throwing motion, he also squeezes the glove and brings it directly back to his chest simultaneously. Partner holds his hand at shoulder height.

Reach back, palm out  The Finish

C. <u>Rocker:</u> Assume the position as if you are throwing to the plate. Partner stands ahead at 6' and holds his hand out and at waist height .
   i. Spread the legs very wide apart (as wide as you would be when landing at release point).
   ii. Place throwing hand (with towel) inside of glove and bring to chest height.
   iii. Begin shifting your weight evenly (rocking) from front leg to back leg 3 times.
   iv. On the third rocker, push off from the back leg as you shift your weight forward while bringing throwing hand/towel around in a quick pitching motion, snap your partners hand with the towel.

Rock forward, then back  The Finish

4. <u>**Knee Drills**</u>: Throw from one knee to a partner for a warm-up, but also to allow for equal and opposite balance through the throwing motion.
   A.   Throw ten times with a two-seam grip (fingers placed along the narrow part of the seams).
   B.   Throw ten times with a four-seam grip (fingers placed across the seams on the ball) – most common way to throw a baseball with little or no movement.  Position players are taught to throw with this type of grip.

**_DRILL PRACTICE:_** _partner is 30' away, throw the baseball using good throwing technique.  This is a warm-up, do not overthrow._

| Knee-Throwing with a Partner | Four-Seam Grip | Two-Seam Grip |

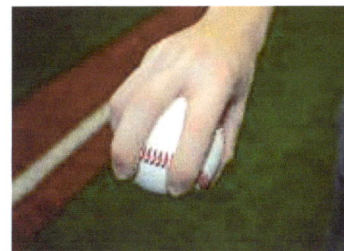

5. <u>**Step Behinds:**</u>
   A.   Player stands up with the front shoulder facing the target, in the set position with glove up and ball inside with throwing hand gripping it.
   B.   In a fluid walking motion, move back leg forward while stepping behind "the pump" leg.  Pump and throw to target.  It is essential to continue proper form and mechanics throughout the delivery.

**_DRILL PRACTICE:_** _Partner stands 70' away (high school) and 50' away (little league); player is to throw both two-seam and four-seam grips to partner, (eight reps)._

Step behind

6. <u>**Bullpen/Flat Ground Throwing**</u>
   A.   Bullpen is as live as possible, throw at proper distance with a catcher in the seated position.
   B.   Work two-seam fastballs on ball side of the plate, and four-seam fastball on opposite side of plate.
   C.   20-30 pitches of early season bullpen is best for the arm.

**_DRILL PRACTICE:_** _Throw a bullpen session to a catcher.  Early in season, throw at 80% speed and increase as training progresses towards the baseball season._

7. <u>**Cool Down**</u>
   A.   Player should run/jog for five minutes, walk for five minutes, run for ten minutes, and finish by walking for five minutes.
   B.   Bike option: ride bike for fifteen minutes.

# Base Running Techniques and Drills

## 1. Home to First:

A. Ground ball on the infield: Sprint hard THROUGH first base. After touching the base, look in foul territory in case of an overthrow. *(For youth players on 60' bases or for high school players on 90' bases: 4.0 seconds or under is a number to work towards as this is considered to be a fast base runner.)*

B. Ball that is hit to the outfield: Sprint hard down the line, making a wide round as you approach first base, step on first base with your right foot and take three hard steps towards second. If outfielder has the ball, get back to first. If the ball is hit into the gap, continue to second base.

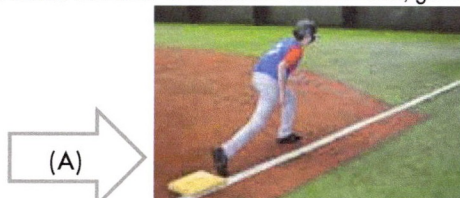

(A)

(B)

**DRILL PRACTICE:** *Running hard and through first base.*   *Then practice a ball hit to the outfield and rounding first.*

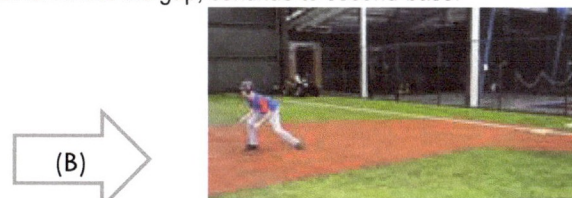

## 2. Proper Lead-Off: *(For levels where stealing is permitted)*

A. While standing on the base, look to the coach for the sign. As you take your lead, eyes need to be fixed on the pitcher's back foot that is in contact with the rubber. Do not take your eyes off the pitcher even for a second!

B. While leaving the base, cross over (left leg over right leg), and then a shuffle, and then another shuffle. This will bring you to a good lead off distance from the base, yet at a safe distance to get back quickly. The crossover, shuffle, shuffle, is designed as a way to measure a lead-off without having the player look down or away from the pitcher to see how far off the base he is.

**DRILL PRACTICE:** *get the sign while on the base, and then crossover, shuffle, shuffle while eyes are on the pitcher.*

## 3. Proper Base Running Stance: *(For age levels where lead-off's are not permitted, use this stance with the left foot against the base)*

A. Eyes fixed on the pitcher's back foot, feet spread wider than shoulders with the toes pointed forward, knees bent and butt down. Hands held up and in front ready to lead the body and assist in take-off.

**DRILL PRACTICE:** *practice the stance position, be able to get good traction as you take off for the next base.*

(2) Lead off Stance

(3) Lead off from base

## 4. Take-Off (Stealing): *(For age groups where stealing is permitted)*

A. Have 70% of your weight on lead leg, as pitcher's first move goes to the plate (or in some leagues, when ball crosses the plate).

B. Explode: push off on left leg crossing over your right leg as you sprint to the base. Be sure to slide properly into the base.
   ***DRILL PRACTICE:*** *practice the explode, push off, cross over, and sprint hard, slide properly into the base, (four reps).*

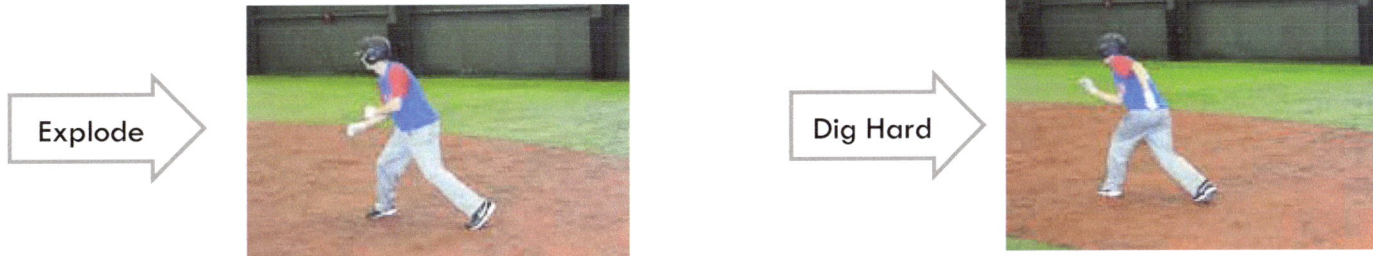

Explode

Dig Hard

## 5. Running from First to Third Base:

A. On a base hit to the outfield, runner break towards second base. Approaching second base the runner is to take a look at the ball (if ball is in LF) or pick up the signal from the third base coach (if ball is in RF), then hit the base with your right foot as you dig for third base.

B. If third base coach has his hands up, player needs to stop and stay on second base.
   ***DRILL PRACTICE:*** *Run the drill and be sure to pick up the coach, (four reps).*

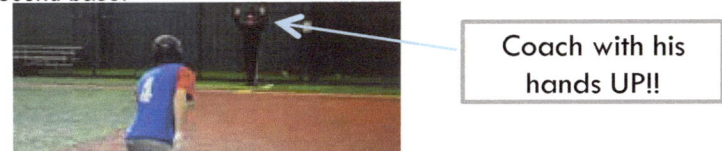

Coach with his hands UP!!

## 6. Sliding Technique:

A. Be sure to slide into the base, NOT on it.

B. Jump into the feet first slide by landing with right leg under left leg. Hold hands high in the air to avoid a hand/wrist jam.
   ***DRILL PRACTICE:*** *slide having players use a blue tarp to slide on, place tarp in front of base. Players should land on the tarp and slide into the base.*

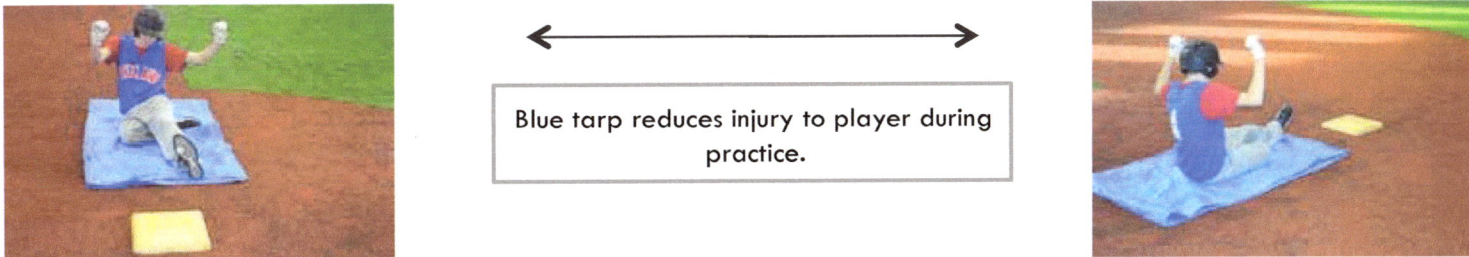

Blue tarp reduces injury to player during practice.

## 7. Hit and Run:

A. Base runner steals and breaks for the next base. Half way to the next base, "peek in" to see what the hitter has done.
   *Example:* If hitter hits a pop up or fly ball, retreat to the previous base. If hitter hits a ground ball or base hit, continue running.

B. Hitter: Must swing at the pitch thrown, even if it is a ball, to protect the runner and hopefully to get a hit and move the runner up two bases.
   ***DRILL PRACTICE:*** *Set up a live situation, have hitters hit and base runners execute their steals and "peek ins".*

# Throwing Techniques and Drills

## 1. General Throwing Technique:

A. Fix eyes fixed on the chest of your partner (target).
B. Grip with a four-seam grip (fingers placed across the seams on the ball) – most common way to throw a baseball with little or no movement. Position players are taught to throw with this type of grip.
C. Take a step or stride towards your target, as you separate the hand and ball from the glove.
D. Extend or reach towards partner with the glove, while bringing ball down and around up to ear.
E. Deliver a strong throw to the target (partner).

## 2. When Receiving the Ball Back from the Partner:

A. Practice using two hands as you look the ball all the way into the glove.
B. Playing catch is a great time to focus on the basics of catching and throwing.

## 3. Throwing Drills: *(DRILL PRACTICE in partners)*

A. Throw from one knee at 50% arm speed, kneel on throwing side knee, glove side knee should be out far enough so that as the throw is completed the chin ends up over the knee. Partner distance 20'.

B. Stand up and square the chest to your partner, rotation at the hips, and at 50% arm speed – throw the ball. Partner distance: 20'.

Square to partner

Rotate hips

**(Throwing Drills Continued)**

    C.   Normal throwing at 75% arm speed.
        -    Step towards your partner hitting him in the chest.  Partner distance: 50' and a rep of ten throws.
    D.   Normal throwing at 80% arm speed.
        - Partner distance: 80' and a rep of ten throws.
    E.   Quarterback Drill: *Use to begin long toss!*
        *Player assumes the position of a football quarter back receiving the snap. The player will drop back five steps and then step forward into the Long Toss throw, be sure to push off hard with the right foot (for right-handers).  Keep the body on one plane, (ten reps).*

Quarterback drill – start                Quarterback drill – drop back

    F.  LONG TOSS:  At 80%-90% arm speed
        i.    Use a "crow hop" to assist in getting the ball to your partner at this distance, (five to seven reps).
        ii.   Partner distance: 200'+ (13-18yr olds), 125' (11-12yr olds), 90' (8-10yr olds), use judgment for player's ability level (4-7yr olds).
    G.  Normal throwing at 100% arm speed . Partner distance: 90' HS, 60' Little League (five to seven reps).

## 4.  Cool Down

    A.   Player should run/jog for five minutes, walk for five minutes, run for ten minutes, and finish by walking for five minutes.
    B.   Bike option: ride bike for fifteen minutes.

"Things turn out best for people who make the best of the way things turn out."

# INDIVIDUAL PRACTICE PLANS

Whether you are a new coach or have coached before, the pressure to provide a good, solid practice is a point of intimidation every year. Maybe you find yourself coaching a team of beginners who just want to have a good experience, or perhaps there is one true "hotshot" player and his dad is putting some pressure on you to help him develop. Either way, you need to have a good plan. I think the most important part of planning a practice is incorporating the technical skills and drills into a fun practice setting that the kids will enjoy. I tend to start by making practice active. There is very little down time for the kids, because typically when kids get bored they lose their focus for the practice session and eventually end up leaving the sport of baseball because, "It seemed too boring." This is a mistake coaches often make and we need to eliminate it. Keep them active and having fun!

# Practice Makes Perfect

*"The doors to success open with a push – just try."*

To effectively run a good practice you need to have a clear objective of what you want the kids to work on. Develop a plan, or use the plans provided in this book to help you and the team accomplish your objective. Baseball is a sport with many different facets to the game. Do not feel that you have to cover every area, every single day in order to be a good coach. Typically, Youth Leagues will reserve one-and-a-half hour time slots for team practices, and it will be impossible to create a practice plan that teaches all the facets within this time frame. As a coach, if you do try to cram all the content into this period you will overwhelm the kids and they will not have enough time to practice it the right way and with reinforcement. You may tend to feel frustrated with this. Instead, lay out a schedule that covers four practices, with the topic areas of focus for each one of those practices. If, in a given practice, you desire extra batting practice, pitching, and infield work, then structure your practice in these areas, and do not be distracted by what you are not working on for that day.

Every coach wants his players to "buy into" what is being taught. If players perceive the coach as an organized person who keeps practices moving and teaches even some of the basic skills in a confident way, the kids will look to you as credible source of instruction. If you tend to let practice happen without preparing, and the kids see you doubting or unsure of what to do next, kids will see you as a non-credible source. The old adage, "You are a product of your own preparation" is so true. Spend time using the plans that are created for you in this section or use them to guide your current practice outline. Making a beautiful first impression with the parents of your players is also a huge key to your season. After all, they need to support you and buy into what you are teaching as well. I have created a pre-season parent letter that you can use as a template for your first letter home to the parents as you kick off the season. The best tip I can offer for speaking to parents or your players is to be very confident in what you say. Be assertive and offer no glimpse of doubt. Coaches need respect in order for everything to be in synch, and being confident in your talk is a great first impression.

Regardless of whether you have coached before or not, there will be some anxiety as you take control of a group of kids. Typically, at the high-school level and higher, coaches are trained educators and individuals who have a deep background and understanding of higher-level baseball. High school and college coaches handle situations and manage teams in an arena that is vastly different than that of a Youth League coach. At the Youth League level, often times the coaches are parents of the kids on the team. Father's who volunteer for coaching Youth League teams typically work full time jobs, and have to manage raising kids and tending to the chores around the house. Their lives are busy. This is why I have created this section of practice plans. I have created a practice notes section mainly to aid in keeping thoughts for practice organized. This form is designed to be a guide for you to use or to recreate to fit your needs. The practice plans are set up to be a very effective and organized means to deliver a practice. The structure is very easy to use with Youth League players and teams, but is the same structure that many high school and college teams use when conducting their practices.

# Practice Plan: Hitting/Pitching

**BASEBALL** CONCEPTS

"We must find a way or make one."

## HITTING

**Forty-Five Minutes: drills are on pages 35-38**

1. **Rotational Warm-up** *(ten minutes)*

2. **T-Drills**
   - ☐ Small bat drill (twelve reps and pick up balls)
   - ☐ Top Half Drill (twelve reps and pick up balls)

3. **Soft Toss**
   - ☐ No stride – work on the load (twelve swings and pick up balls)
   - ☐ With stride (twelve swings and pick up balls)
   - ☐ With stride, toss from behind (twelve swings and pick up balls)

4. **Cage Hitting**
   - ☐ Full swing, practice proper techniques (ten swings MAX, rest, and then seven more swings) PICK UP BALLS
   - ☐ Cage hitting with stride, try to hit ball back up the middle (ten swings MAX, rest, and then seven more swings) PICK UP BALLS

5. **Body Work** *(ten minutes)*

## PITCHING

**Forty-Five Minutes: drills are on pages 39-41**

1. **Rotational Warm –up** *(ten minutes)*

2. **Throw "Get Loose"**
   - ☐ Knee throwing at 50% arm speed (ten throws) **Distance: 20'.**
   - ☐ Step behinds and pump knee (ten throws) **Distance: 60'.**
   - ☐ Quarterback drill: Drop back, step up, get your momentum moving forward, and throw the baseball to your target, (seven throws).

3. **Bullpen**
   - ☐ On mound (or flat ground): two-seam and four-seam fast balls (ten pitches each).
   - ☐ Throw to a catcher who is seated in the catching position. For a right-handed pitcher, throw the two-seam on the INSIDE corner of the plate to a righty and four-seam to the OUTSIDE.

4. **Towel Drills**
   - ☐ Stacked, Rocker, Against Wall, and stride plus five, (ten reps of each).

5. **Cool Down and Body Work** *(ten minutes)*

# Practice Plan: Throwing/Base Running

**BASEBALL CONCEPTS**

> "It isn't the plays or the system that gets the job done, it's the quality of the people in the system."

## BASERUNNING

Thirty-Five Minutes: drills are on pages 42-43

1. **Rotational Warm-up** *(ten minutes)*

2. **Base Running Practice**

   - Running hard through first base and after touching the base, look in foul territory in case of an over throw. (four reps) Use a stopwatch and time the firsts and fourth rep. *(For youth players on 60' bases or for high school players on 90' bases: 4.0 seconds or under is a number to work towards as this is considered to be a fast base runner.)*

   - Run hard from home and round 1st base on a single, (4 reps).

3. **Lead Off and Stealing**

   - Lead-off's: Eyes on pitcher - Cross over, shuffle, shuffle, (five reps).

   - Secondary Lead: Hop, Hop, Hop, Go, (five reps).

   - Stealing: Exploding by pushing off with left leg crossing over right leg (three reps).

4. **Sliding**

   - Pop Up Sliding Drill: hands in the air while sliding into base and popping up. *Use blue tarp for safety,* (six reps).

5. **Bodywork and Cool Down** *(fifteen minutes)*

## THROWING

Forty Minutes: drills are on pages 44-45

1. **Rotational Warm –up** *(fifteen minutes)*

2. **Throw to "Get Loose"**

   - Throwing from one knee at 50% arm speed. **Distance: 20'** (thirteen throws).

   - Stand up, square chest to partner, rotation at the waist at 50% arm speed. **Distance: 20'** (thirteen throws).

3. **Normal Throwing "Play Catch"**

   - 75% arm speed: Step towards partner, throw- aiming for the chest. When receiving baseball, use two hands, (ten throws) **Distance: 50'.**

   - Normal throwing at 80% arm speed, (ten throws) **Distance: 80'.**

4. **LONG TOSS**

   - At 80%-90% arm speed, (ten throws), **Distance:** 200' High School, 125' (11-12yr olds), 100' (8-10 yr olds), use judgment for player's ability level (4-7yr olds).

   - Normal throwing at 100% arm speed, (three throws), **Distance:** 70' HS, 50' Little League.

5. **Cool Down and Body Work** *(ten minutes)*

*Note that the key to this throwing session is the gradual progression of strengthening the arm. The player is to ease into the work out and going only to his limit, only the player will be able to tell the limit based on how his arm feels. Do not overwork the arm if it is hurting or tight.*

# Practice Plan: Fielding

**BASEBALL** CONCEPTS

*"If you do the right thing every time, you will please most people, and astonish others."*

## OUTFIELDING

Forty-Five Minutes: drills are on pages 32-34

1. **Rotational Warm-up** *(ten minutes)*

2. **Throw "Get Loose"**
   - Soft catch from knees 25' apart (eleven throws).
   - 60' toss (eleven throws).
   - 90' toss (eleven throws).

3. **Drills**
   - Tweener Drill (ten reps).
   - Over the shoulder catches (ten reps).
   - Hit Ground balls with *crow hops* (ten reps).
   - Staying behind a fly ball and coming through it as a base runner is tagging up (eight reps). Set up a sock net or a bucket as a target for the throw to go into. This is fun for the kids!

4. **Hit or Throw Fly Balls**
   - The player practices running to the spot and catching a fly ball with two hands.

5. **Body work and Cool Down** *(ten minutes)*

## INFIELDING

Forty-Five Minutes: drills are on pages 27-31

1. **Rotational Warm-up** *(ten minutes)*

2. **Throw "Get Loose"**
   - Soft catch from knees 25' apart (eleven throws), 60' toss (eleven throws), and 90' toss (eleven throws).

3. **Drills**
   - Shuffle drill (fifteen rolls).
   - Short-hop drill "Scoops": In front, back hand, and glove side (ten hops per position).
   - Ready step approach (with out the ball).
   - Fielding a ground ball. Ready step, right – left, extend, two hands, thumb to thumb. Roll and hit the balls to the player.

4. **Hit Ground balls to players** *(twenty-five reps of each)*
   - Practice repetition: fielding and throwing.
   - Practice repetition: starting a double play.
   - Practice repetition: turning the double play. Ease up on the throws for arm safety.

5. **Cool down and body work** *(fifteen minutes)*

# Practice Plan: Situations

> "He who is good at making excuses is seldom good for anything else."

## HITTING "Small Ball"

*Forty-Five Minutes: drills are on page 30*

1. **Rotational Warm up** *(ten minutes)*

2. **Bunting in the cage**
   - Bunting to first base side (ten bunts).
   - Bunting to third base side (ten bunts).
   - Squeeze bunts (ten bunts).
   - Bunting for a hit (ten bunts).

3. **T-work**
   - Hitting the ball to right field (fifteen swings).

4. **Soft toss**
   - Hitting the ball to right field (ten swings).

5. **In cage**
   - Live Arm: Hitting ball to right field, drive hands through the zone first.

6. **Body Work** *(ten minutes)*

## PITCHERS "Fielding Practice"

*Forty-Five Minutes: use fielding techniques on page 20*

1. **Rotational Warm-up** *(ten minutes)*

2. **Hit Ground Balls to Pitcher (on mound)**
   - To right side of mound, throw to first (five reps).
   - Straight on, hit right back to mound, throw to first (five reps).
   - To left side of mound, throw to first (five reps).

3. **Hit ground balls to Pitcher (on mound)**
   - To the right side, start a double play at second, SS is covering, (five reps).
   - Straight on, hit back to mound,, start a DP at second, SS is covering, (five reps).
   - To left side, start a DP at second, SS is covering (five reps).

4. **Pitcher's covering first base on ball hit to right side**
   - Run up first base line, catch ball, then step on the inside edge of the base in stride. Peel off away from the base runner.

5. **Bunt balls back to the pitcher (on mound)**
   - Bunt balls to the pitcher - right, left, and straight on), (five reps of each).

6. **Body work and Cool down** *(fifteen minutes)*.

51

# Practice Plan: Catching/"Little Things"

**"It's not hard to make decisions when you know what your values are."**

## CATCHING

### Forty-Five Minutes: drills are on pages 23-26

1. **Rotational Warm-up** *(ten minutes)*

2. **Proper Stance**
   - Signal Stance, Receiving Stance, Man on Stance.

3. **Receiving & Framing**
   - Bare hand, receiving and framing, (ten reps).
   - With glove, receiving and framing, (ten reps).

4. **Blocking a Pitch in the dirt**
   - The Gauntlet drill, (five to eight reps).
   - Throwing the balls in the dirt, (ten to fifteen reps).

5. **Blocking the Plate from base runner**
   - Find the plate, receive the ball, and brace for impact.

6. **Footwork and Throwing**
   - Practice footwork and throwing the ball to the each base.

7. **Cool Down and Body Work** *(ten minutes)*

## COACHING "The Little Things"

### Thirty Minutes: drills are on page 22

1. **Scouting the opponent – Pre game**
   - Practice having players stand in single file outside the dugout and watching the other team warm-up.

2. **Taking the field – Hustle Drill!**
   - Have players sprint to their positions (under ten seconds).
   - Centerfielder and first baseman take practice ball with them.
   - Players must talk and "chatter" while in the field.

3. **Player's picking each other up**
   - Base runners that make the final out of inning, defensive players returning to the field need to run his glove and hat out to him. This speeds up the game!

4. **On deck batter**
   - For a play at the plate, tell the base runner coming from third to slide or stand up by using arm motions, up or down.
   - Assist the umpire in retrieving a foul ball to the back stop.

5. **Positive Quote**
   - State the positive quote (coach's choice) and talk of its importance and how the kids can put this into use in their lives and on the baseball field.

# Practice Notes

"Bad language promotes poor sportsmanship."

## Practice Notes

Practice Time: _____

Asst. Coaches: _____

*Warm-up:* _____

*Throwing:* _____

*Hitting:* _____

*Pitching:* _____

*Outfield:* _____

*Infield:* _____

*BaseRun:* _____

*Players:* _____

*Groups:* _____

*Quote:* _____

## For the next practice

Practice Time: _____

Asst. Coaches: _____

_____

_____

_____

_____

_____

_____

_____

_____

_____

_____

# Full Team Practice Plans

**BASEBALL** CONCEPTS

## 1 1/2 Hour Long Practice Time

### 1. WARM-UP Rotational Warm-up and Running *(Whole Team) TEN MINS*

### 2. THROW to "Get Loose" (Whole Team) TEN MINS

- Throwing from one knee at 50% arm speed, (thirteen throws) **Distance: 20'.**
- Stand up, square chest to partner, rotation at the waist at 50% arm speed, (thirteen throws) Distance: 20'.

#### Normal Throwing "Play Catch" (*Whole Team*)

- 75% arm speed: step towards partner and throw at his chest. When receiving the baseball, use two hands (ten throws) **Distance: 50'.**
- Normal throwing at 80% arm speed (ten throws) **Distance: 80'.**

### 3. HITTING T-Drills: *Start with ½ team with one coach,* FIFTEEN MINS then Rotate Groups

- One hand, small bat drill (six reps and pick up balls).
- Top Half Drill (six reps and pick up balls).

#### Soft Toss:

- No stride - work on the load, (six swings and pick up balls).
- With stride, (six swings and pick up balls).
- With stride - toss from behind, (twelve swings and pick up balls).

#### Cage Hitting:

- Practice proper techniques (six swings MAX, rest, and then six more swings), PICK UP BALLS.
- Cage hitting with stride, try to hit ball back up the middle (six swings MAX, rest, and then six more swings), PICK UP BALLS.

### 4. INFIELDING Drills: *Other ½ of team with a coach,15 MINS then Rotate*

- Shuffle drill, (fifteen rolls).
- Short-hop drill "Scoops": In front, back hand, and glove side, (fifteen hops per position).
- Ready step approach, (with out ball).
- Fielding ground balls. Ready step, right – left, extend, two hands, thumb to thumb. Roll and hit balls to the player.

#### Hit Ground balls to players:

- Practice repetition: fielding and throwing.
- Practice repetition: starting a double play.
- Practice repetition: turning the double play.

### 5. BASE RUNNING Practice: *(Whole Team, in two groups) TEN MINS*

- Running hard through first base. After touching base, look in foul territory in case of an overthrow, (3 reps). Use a stopwatch to time the first and second reps.
- Running hard and rounding first base on a single, (four reps).
- Run from first to third base, practice picking up the 3B coach!

#### Sliding:

- Pop Up Sliding Drill: hands in the air while sliding into the base and popping up. *Use blue tarp for safety,* (six reps).

### 6. BODYWORK and Cool Down *(five minutes)*

# Choosing a Bat and Glove Size

How to choose a <u>bat</u> and <u>glove</u> that fits you?

**Determine Your Bat Length by Weight and Height**

| Your weight (pounds) | Your height (inches) | | | | | | | | | |
|---|---|---|---|---|---|---|---|---|---|---|
| | 36-40 | 41-44 | 45-48 | 49-52 | 53-56 | 57-60 | 61-64 | 65-68 | 69-72 | 73+ |
| | **Bat length** | | | | | | | | | |
| less than 60 | 26" | 27" | 28" | 29" | 29" | | | | | |
| 61-70 | 27" | 27" | 28" | 29" | 30" | 30" | | | | |
| 71-80 | | 28" | 28" | 29" | 30" | 30" | 31" | | | |
| 81-90 | | 28" | 29" | 29" | 30" | 30" | 31" | 32" | | |
| 91-100 | | 28" | 29" | 30" | 30" | 31" | 31" | 32" | | |
| 101-110 | | 29" | 29" | 30" | 30" | 31" | 31" | 32" | | |
| 111-120 | | 29" | 29" | 30" | 30" | 31" | 31" | 32" | | |
| 121-130 | | 29" | 29" | 30" | 30" | 31" | 32" | 33" | 33" | |
| 131-140 | | 29" | 30" | 30" | 31" | 31" | 32" | 33" | 33" | |
| 141-150 | | | 30" | 30" | 31" | 31" | 32" | 33" | 33" | |
| 151-160 | | | 30" | 31" | 31" | 32" | 32" | 33" | 33" | 33" |
| 161-170 | | | | 31" | 31" | 32" | 32" | 33" | 33" | 34" |
| 171-180 | | | | | | 32" | 33" | 33" | 34" | 34" |
| 180+ | | | | | | | 33" | 33" | 34" | 34" |

**Most popular by size**

| AGE | 5 to 7 | 8 to 9 | 10 | 11 to 12 | 13 to 14 | 15 to 18 |
|---|---|---|---|---|---|---|
| LENGTH | 24"-26" | 26"-28" | 28"-29" | 30"-31" | 31"-32" | 32"-33" |

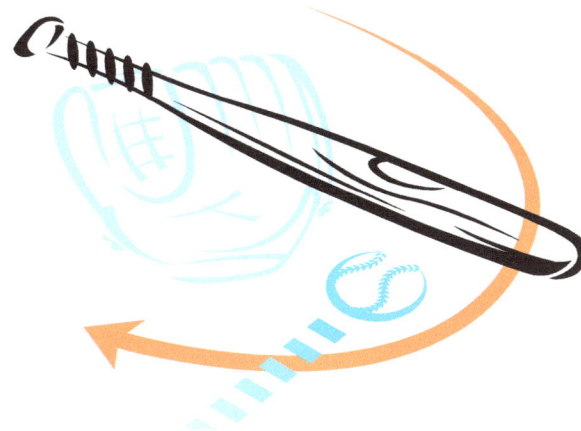

**Determining Your Glove Size**

| Age | Position | Glove size |
|---|---|---|
| Under 8 | Infield | 9" |
| Under 8 | Outfield | 11" |
| 9 to 13 | Infield | 9-10" |
| 9 to 13 | Outfield | 11-12" |
| High School/Adult | Infield | 10 1/2-11 1/2" |
| High School/Adult | Outfield | 12-12 1/2" |

# Positive Quotes...

**BASEBALL CONCEPTS**

*I can do everything through Him who gives me strength.* *Philippians 4:13*

## ATTITUDE

Things turn out best for people who make the best of the way things turn out.
*-John Wooden*

Remember, you meet your opponents, not their reputation.
*-Anonymous*

Men are not prisoners of fate, but only prisoners of their own minds.
*-Franklin D. Roosevelt*

A positive attitude is not a destination – it's a way of life.
*-Anonymous*

Whether you think you can or think you can't – you're right!
*-Henry Ford*

## DETERMINATION

The key to success is to climb the ladder instead of waiting for the elevator.
*-Anonymous*

The doors to success open with a push – just try.
*-Anonymous*

We must find a way or make one.
*-Hannibal*

## CHARACTER

It isn't the plays or the system that gets the job done, it's the quality of the people in the system.
*-Joe Paterno*

If you do the right thing every time, you will please most people, and astonish others.
*-Anonymous*

He who is good at making excuses is seldom good for anything else.
*-Benjamin Franklin*

It's not hard to make decisions when you know what your values are.
*-Anonymous*

Bad language promotes poor sportsmanship.
*-Kenneth Kladnik*

## DISCIPLINE

The hot games are won by those with cool heads.
*-Anonymous*

Few men are born brave; many have become so through training and force of discipline.
*--Vegetius*

Remember that winners do what loser don't want to.
*-Anonymous*

### Coach Jeff VanHuis M.Ed.

Coach Jeff VanHuis has over sixteen years of baseball experience both as a player and as a coach. After finishing high school, he spent three seasons playing Division II collegiate baseball at Ferris State University and was named team co-captain as a junior. He also spent two seasons playing city majors travel baseball before entering the coaching ranks. Coach VanHuis has nine years of experience coaching high school varsity baseball. As a teacher, he has taught eight years at the high school and middle school level. His master's degree in education has allowed him to develop baseball skills curriculum and teach over seven hundred baseball players in a variety of camp, practice, and game settings. Coach VanHuis is a member of both the Michigan and American baseball coaches' associations. His affiliation with major colleges and universities has helped in promoting and assisting many youth players to reach their high school and college baseball goals. He has also coached at the Youth League level providing him with a first-hand glimpse of what resources kids, parents, and coaches at this level need. Each year, Coach VanHuis instructs skills camps ranging from four-year-old t-ball camps to high school developmental camps. He is currently the head varsity coach at Zeeland West High School in Zeeland, Michigan.

This coach's guidebook has been developed because Coach VanHuis sees such an opportunity for positive influence that Youth League baseball can provide. He wants to equip coaches with sound instructional resources so they can make the most of this opportunity. Youth League baseball is a great American event, which almost every youngster is involved with at some point. Let's make it a wonderful, fun, and rewarding time for them! Coach VanHuis says, "My son Caden is a Youth Leaguer, and I want the best possible learning experience for him and kids like him. This mindset has paved the way for the creation of this phenomenal coaches' guide. Kids deserve the best and the adults in their lives have the responsibility to help them to develop and be the best they can be in a healthy way. I have a passion for Youth League baseball and for kids to positively benefit from involvement in it. I firmly believe that coaches and parents are the key, so here is a tool for them."

Baseball Concepts offers coaching consulting to Youth League and youth baseball associations. We have worked with a number of youth coaches through clinics and speaking engagements. Visit www.baseball-concepts.com, where parents and coaches can read valuable information pertaining to parenting their child through sports, allowing kids to be kids, and also some very useful information if you do find yourself coaching your child's baseball team.

**Coach Jeff VanHuis
and his son Caden**

## ABOUT THE AUTHOR

"Nothing gives one person so much advantage over another as to remain always cool and unruffled under all circumstances." - Thomas Jefferson

### Stu Fritz – Hope College Head Baseball Coach
- Eight-Time DIII MIAA Conference Champion Coach, Hope College, Holland, MI
- Four appearances in the NCAA National Championships
- Hope College All-Time most wins as coach

### Bill Curtis – Los Angeles Angels and Forest Hills Eastern High School Coach
Grand Canyon University (DI) 1997-99
- All-American 2nd Team 1999
- Conference Player of the Year 1999
- Regional Player of the Year 1999

Drafted by Anaheim Angels 1999
- Anaheim Angels 1999 - 2002
- Highest level - Single A (Midwest League)

Currently
- MLB Advance scout for Inside Edge
- Varsity Coach Forest Hills Eastern HS
- International baseball clinician (conducts annual clinics in Thailand and Italy as well as various sites around the US)

### Tony DiLaura – Calvin College
- Former DIII MIAA All-Conference Catcher, Calvin College, Grand Rapids, MI
- Three-Time MHSAA District Champion Coach, South Christian High School, MI

### Brandon Haveman – Purdue University and Seattle Mariners
- 2nd team All –Big Ten (2008)
- 1st team All-Big Ten (2009)
- All-Time Career batting average leader at Purdue
- 2-time Big Ten Batting Champion (2008-2009)
- Drafted Seattle Mariners in June of 2009
- Appalachian League Rookie All Star (2009)

# ADVISORY BOARD MEMBERS

This Baseball Concepts Coaches Guide has been developed with the professional counsel of the advisory board. The advisors of this product have extensive experience in both playing and coaching baseball at many different levels. This group has combined to produce this extremely effective baseball coaching tool. Their expertise has helped parents and coaches in Youth League cities across the world. The advisory team and their wealth of experience can guarantee a solid baseball instructional product!

Baseball Concepts' mission is to truly aid in the improvement of the youth baseball experience for kids, parents, and coaches. This is accomplished through methods that include baseball camps, consulting, speaking with Youth Leaguers, their parents, and their coaches. Our signature event is the father/son style baseball camp and events that bring dads and their kids together. In addition to the father/son camp, we teach advanced skills through a variety of camps for youth players that share the fundamental principals of the game of baseball. There is also a large dose of emphasis on how to be successful in just being a great person and not worrying about what others think. Our coaches' clinics show coaches the specific drills and techniques needed to run a great practice while giving kids the skills needed to have a great baseball season. The message that can be easily overlooked is this: creative ways do exist to steer kids in the right direction for success in life through the way that you coach. Understand that you do have a profound impact on the way these kids will think about themselves and how this will shape their future.  Thanks for being a great dad who devotes time to using this book as you spend time with your kids!

Coaches' clinics quite often overlook giving coaches the confidence to show young boys how to be good men. This is really the core of our job as adults! When speaking at Youth League events or to youth baseball parents, we relish the opportunity to talk about the big things about baseball that can bring families together and give coaches a sense of accomplishment even when coaching a team where the wins are hard to get.

I have devoted a section of our website (www.baseball-concepts.com) to giving parents healthy ideas and tips on how they can help their kids in the game of baseball and in life. I encourage parents and coaches to use this as a resource, and to discover some refreshing, new ideas on how to make a difference with your child. To bring a Baseball Concepts skills camp to your local Youth League or to speak at a community baseball event in your town, please contact us for more information.

# ADDITIONAL RESOURCES

Baseball Concepts LLC, Zeeland, MI
Website: **www.baseball-concepts.com**
Email address: **jeff@baseball-concepts.com**

www.ingramcontent.com/pod-product-compliance
Lightning Source LLC
Chambersburg PA
CBHW061056090426
42742CB00002B/61

*9780982444634*